Unwavering

Unwavering

Living with *Defiant* JOY

STUDY GUIDE | SIX SESSIONS

STASI ELDREDGE

NELSON
BOOKS

An Imprint of Thomas Nelson

RANSOMED HEART
LOVE GOD. LIVE FREE.
RANSOMEDHEART.COM

Published in Nashville, Tennessee, by Nelson Books, an imprint of Thomas Nelson. Nelson Books and Thomas Nelson are registered trademarks of HarperCollins Christian Publishing, Inc.

Published in association with Yates & Yates, www.yates2.com.

Thomas Nelson titles may be purchased in bulk for educational, business, fund-raising, or sales promotional use. For information, please e-mail SpecialMarkets@ ThomasNelson.com.

ISBN 978-0-310-09690-0

First Printing August 2018 / Printed in the United States of America

Contents

SESSION 1

A Reason to Celebrate

INTRODUCTION

Group leader reads aloud these opening words from Stasi:

I love to celebrate. I love birthday parties and baby showers, holidays and homecomings. But I especially love Christmas. Except when I don't. At the beginning of too many holiday seasons, I can become overwhelmed by what is "required" of me. That is, I did, until I needed to pare down for my sanity's sake and to also keep my family from hiding from me. Still, I love creating spaces for beauty and for others' lives to be honored. And honestly, there's no one I love to honor more than our Jesus, and gathering to celebrate Him brings me the greatest joy.

But life doesn't take holidays. Pain doesn't check out. World events don't slow down. Evil doesn't give vacations. So how do we become a people who learn to celebrate the goodness of God and His many gifts in the midst of what is often a heartbreaking world? How do we grow to be a people known for our unwavering joy right in the middle of our hurting world?

Let's press in to find out together.

WATCH VIDEO SESSION 1

Video Notes

Use this space to make note of anything that stands out to you in the teaching.

"Weeping may stay for the night, but rejoicing comes in the morning."
(Psalm 30:5)

GROUP DISCUSSION: "DEFIANCE"

Gather into small groups if part of a larger group. Spend time together reacting to what Stasi said in the video through these prompts and questions.

Gathering Together

Read aloud as a group the following Scripture:

"I consider that our present sufferings are not worth comparing with the glory that will be revealed in us." (Romans 8:18)

What jumped out at you or surprised you or struck you most in the video?

1. Stasi said defiance means resistance, opposition, noncompliance, disobedience, dissent, and rebellion. How do you feel about associating this definition with the living God?

2. When it comes to things that would destroy our souls, do you agree or disagree that this is the right response? Why or why not?

3. We oppose death and destruction by the life of Christ in us. We dissent by casting our vote against the belief that sorrow and endless suffering win. We welcome life, love, and the full work of Christ to bring all of His goodness into every aspect of our and His domains.

   Brainstorm together some words you could use to fill in these blanks and briefly discuss what it means to actively oppose death through the life of Christ in us:

   We comply with _____.

   We obey _____.

   We respect His _____ and His _____.

   We overcome evil with _____.

   We defy hatred by embracing _____.

   We dissent by _____.

   We choose _____.

4. Think about the phrase "choose joy." Make a list of what that might look like in your everyday life, and share one idea with the group.

5. Share two or three areas where you would like more joy in your life.

6. Everyone has known seasons of suffering and pain. Every person has a story to tell. Tell about either a past time of suffering or one that you're currently experiencing.

The presence of God is our good. And knowing His presence in the pain is the sweetest gift of all.

7. In the Garden of Gethsemane, Jesus prayed, "My Father, if it be possible, let *this cup* pass from me; nevertheless, not as I will, but as you will" (Matthew 26:39 ESV, emphasis added). What is the *cup* you are asking (or have asked) to pass from you?

   Encourage one another to accept God's will, not our own, in this circumstance.

8. To continue to host the Christmas Party on the evening that the Sandy Hook Elementary School shooting took place, we needed to be honest about our grief and sorrow over the lives lost. We also needed to proclaim that even in the midst of this horrific tragedy, Jesus has triumphed over death.

   Where do you need to proclaim and enforce the victory of Jesus Christ? (Take turns sharing.)
   - In a place you are struggling or fearful
   - Where you are concerned over loved ones lives and choices
   - A particular evil in the world

Scripture Response

Ask for volunteers to read each of the following verses/passages aloud to the group. Go around the room and have each woman share one word or phrase that comes to mind after hearing these Scriptures:

"I have told you these things, so that in me you may have peace. In this world you will have trouble. But take heart! I have overcome the world." (John 16:33)

"The LORD your God is with you,
   the Mighty Warrior who saves.
He will take great delight in you;
   in his love he will no longer rebuke you,
   but will rejoice over you with singing." (Zephaniah 3:17)

"The Spirit himself testifies with our spirit that we are God's children. Now if we are God's children, then we are heirs—heirs of God and co-heirs with Christ, if indeed we share in his sufferings in order that we may share in his glory." (Romans 8:16-17)

Leader reads this final note from Stasi:

Yes, Jesus is known as the Man of Sorrows, but He is also the God of great joy! He rejoices over you. Yes, you. Right now. Our God sees the end from the beginning. When He looks at you, He doesn't see your failures, your disappointments, or even your sins. He looks at you and sees His spotless, perfect, beloved. His favor rests on you. He chose you before the foundation of the earth to belong to Him. You are His child.

We can rejoice over that.

CLOSING PRAYER

Leader or volunteer, close your group time in prayer:

Dear Father,

Thank you that I am Your child. I pray to know You more deeply as my good Father. I pray to encounter Your love increasingly, even in moments and seasons of travail. I need to see life with Your eyes. You know that what is suffered now does not compare to the glory that You will reveal in us. I pray to know that too. Thank You that You will provide everything I need every single day of my life. I pray to know Your Presence in the midst of my every day—the days of celebration and the days of sorrow. Your Name is Faithful and True, and I believe You are for me. Thank You. Thank You.

In Jesus' glorious Name,

Amen

Session 1

Personal Study

Read chapters 1–2 in Defiant Joy. *Then, reread the excerpts included here and answer the questions that follow.*

> *Defiant* may not be a word we would normally associate with the living God, but it can actually be quite fitting. Defiance means resistance, opposition, non-compliance, disobedience, dissent, and rebellion. And when it comes to things which would destroy our souls, that is exactly the right response.
>
> We are called to resist the lies of the enemy. Like Christian in *Pilgrim's Progress*, we do not comply with the Vanity Fair offerings of the world. We are instructed to not obey the clamoring of the flesh. We are urged to rebel against sin. By the life of Christ in us, we oppose death and destruction. We dissent by casting our vote against the belief that sorrow and endless suffering win.
>
> Instead, we welcome life, love, and the full work of Christ to bring all of His goodness into every aspect of our domains and His. We comply with truth. We obey our God. We respect His authority and His final say. We overcome evil with good. We defy hatred by embracing love.
>
> We choose joy.
>
> —*Defiant Joy*, pages 9–10

1. In your own words, how would you describe the difference between happiness and joy?

2. I describe defiance as meaning "resistance, opposition, noncompliance, disobedience, dissent, and rebellion." How would you describe "*defiant* joy"?

3. How would you describe "denial"?

4. How are the two different?

5. Can you remember a time when you were defiantly joyful? What happened?

6. What was the effect of your defiant joy on those around you?

7. I confessed in *Defiant Joy* that I do not think of myself as a naturally joyful person, but others in my life would disagree. One of my favorite words is "YAY!" Where do you land on the spectrum of experiencing joy?

If you asked someone you trusted if they think of you as joyful, what do you think they would say? Want to risk asking them? Pray about that!

We humans are a mystery. We are not meant to be a stranger unto our very selves, but feeling like a stranger in our world, even to those closest to us, is often a commonplace experience.

Feeling alone is a sorrow we share, and being alone is the first thing God named as "not good": "It is not good for the man to be alone" (Gen. 2:18). Yet we do feel alone. Isolated. Not understood and too often not wanted. It is not merely your condition; it is one we all have, and one that we feel compelled to run from. Numb. Escape. Ignore. It is a difficult thing to long for connection and meaning and live under a burden of futility and an emptiness that mocks. But when we run, we seed the fruit of denial and end up increasing our pain rather than soothing it. Hopelessness and denial may temporarily deaden desire and the pain of when it is unmet, but desire is a flame that refuses to be quenched.

—*Defiant Joy*, pages 17–18

8. Are you aware of feeling "outside" of life sometimes? Of feeling lonely? In what ways or circumstances?

We all feel lonely and we feel it often. The truth of Hebrews 13:5 is a great comfort. Take a few minutes to look it up and read it. Sit with this verse for a minute.

9. What comfort does Jesus offer in Hebrews 13:5?

On the night He was betrayed, Jesus did not want to be alone in the Garden but asked His sleepy disciples to stay awake with Him. Though they may have desired to stay awake, they failed Jesus by leaving Him alone in His agony. Jesus understands the feeling of being lonely and even misunderstood. He understands *you*. Your feeling lonely at times is a suffering that Jesus knows very well. It is part of the cup that we drink to share in His sufferings. It can even be something that draws our hearts closer to His.

When the soldiers came to the garden and Jesus stepped forward to offer Himself to His enemies, Peter also stepped forward and cut off the ear of the servant of the high priest. Jesus scolded Peter and told him to put away his sword. Then He asked, "Shall I not drink the cup the Father has given me?" (John 18:11).

What is this cup? Actually, Jesus had mentioned this cup prior to that fateful night.

Earlier in Matthew 20:20–28, the mother of James and John, in typical motherly fashion, asked Jesus whether her nice, upstanding sons could have the honor of sitting beside Him in His kingdom. Jesus answered with a question: "Are you able to drink the cup that I am about to drink?" (Matt. 20:22 NASB).

It was not a rebuke. It was simply a question, to which the brothers replied, "We are able" (Matt. 20:22 NASB).

It was a yes blithely given. Clearly, they couldn't understand the full weight of what Jesus was asking. Jesus then turned to the other disciples who were mad that James and John's mother had presumed to ask such a thing. They wanted to be seated next to Jesus as well.

Jesus spoke to all of them then and said that greatness in the kingdom of God is not easily obtained. It comes along the path of love—a path of sacrifice, service, and suffering. This is the cup of Jesus. And the people who seek to follow in His footsteps must drink of it and become like the one who came "not . . . to be served, but to serve, and to give his life as a ransom for many" (Matt. 20:28).

—*Defiant Joy*, pages 25–26

10. Look up Psalm 30:5b. Write it here.

What does this verse mean to you?

11. Read John 16:22 out loud.

> So you have sorrow now, but I will see you again; then you will rejoice, and no one can rob you of that joy. (John 16:22 NLT)

Next, look up John 16:33. What idea do these two verses share?

Jesus does not promise a life without suffering. He does however promise that suffering will not overcome us. Not only has He suffered on our behalf, winning for us the triumph over death and sorrow, but He is coming again and bringing to us a life where suffering will no longer exist.

There was another cup offered to Jesus at the top of the hill at Golgotha. As He was suffering, the merciful centurion handed Him a cup. Jesus sniffed the liquid. It was wine mixed with myrrh, a mild narcotic to dull the pain. But Jesus knew He was not meant to dull the pain nor numb it in any way. He was to feel it. So He refused to drink the elixir. No denial. No numbing. He endured being fully awake to the pain, so it might produce all of its intended work.

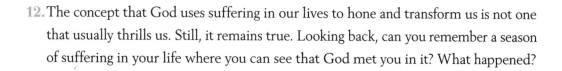

Because Jesus drank from the cup of suffering and wrath, that cup became the cup of salvation. The cup of suffering became the cup of joy. Turns out, it's the same cup.

Hebrews 12 says that it was for the joy that was set before Him that Jesus endured His tortuous death on the cross. But to get to the joy, He first had to be willing to drink the cup of suffering. In the midst of His suffering, Jesus fixed His gaze on His Dad and held on to the joy that He knew was coming to Him on the other side of the cross. He showed us that we, too, can have joy in the midst of our suffering—and no one can it take away from us.

—Defiant Joy, pages 27–28

12. The concept that God uses suffering in our lives to hone and transform us is not one that usually thrills us. Still, it remains true. Looking back, can you remember a season of suffering in your life where you can see that God met you in it? What happened?

13. Look up the following verses and jot down the key point:

John 3:16

Colossians 1:13

Colossians 2:13

Ephesians 2:18

1 Corinthians 15:57

14. In light of what Jesus has accomplished on your behalf, what reasons do you have
to be joyful?

The sorrow and grief that come are real, and we have a God who is well
acquainted with them. He doesn't ask us to ignore our grief but to invite Him
into it that we might bear it together.

No matter what, we can know an internal defiant joy because death has
been defeated. Life has won. There is suffering, yes. But always there is the
potential for joy.

In the face of the ultimate reality won for us by Jesus, we don't have to
pretend that life is better than it is, that we don't hurt as much as we do, or
that we are feeling happy when we are not. We are invited to be fully alive,
awake, alert, oriented to the truth, and to know that because of Jesus, we can
be defiantly joyful.

—*Defiant Joy*, pages 31–32

WORSHIP SONG

I love to worship God. Music is dear to my heart and is one of my favorite ways to help me focus on how marvelous God is and praise Him for all He has done. Each week, I'll be suggesting a few of my favorite worship songs for you to worship to. You can pick any one of them—or all of them! Put it (them) on repeat! Find a time to listen when you are not distracted by many other things. Bless you.

- "Beloved" – Leeland
- "Here" – Kari Jobe
- "It Is Well" – Kristene DiMarco & Bethel Music

CONTEMPLATIVE PRAYER

Contemplative Prayer is a simple practice that has been engaged in by our spiritual fathers and mothers for centuries. It is a tool given to us to help us center all our faculties on the Presence of God in the moment we find ourselves. There are concerns in some Christian circles because the New Age movement has hijacked this practice, and a form of it is used in both Hindu and Buddhist traditions. We will not practice those "techniques." We don't have to be afraid to simply sit in stillness and quiet ourselves before God. We come under His authority and His alone. Mary **pondered** things in her heart (see Luke 2:19). David says, "My eyes stay open through the watches of the night, that I may **meditate** on your promises" (Psalm 119:148). Joshua 1:8 instructs us, "This book of the law shall not depart from your mouth, but you shall **meditate** on it day and night" (NASB).

We, too, want to set our thoughts on those above. We want to saturate our minds and our spirits with the Word of God. Meditating on Scripture is a wise and life-bringing thing to do.

Now, I know that life is swirling. You have a list you have to make. Don't forget that bill you have to pay, that phone call to return, that topic you need to talk about with you-know-who. You know what I mean. To find the time to sit and let go of all those things, even for a few minutes, can feel daunting. Daunting it may be, but it is still well worth it.

Each week, I will invite you to practice Contemplative Prayer. Sometimes we will imagine ourselves in a passage of Scripture and being right there with Jesus in it. Don't think of it as something you have "to do." Think of it as a gift you get to receive. It will be simple.

We'll begin small. Just a few minutes.

Get comfortable.

Wait. Go back and silence your phone. It'll be okay. This is just going to be for five minutes max.

Okay, back to your comfy place.

To begin, you are simply going to "come home" to your body, where Christ dwells within you. Notice what you are feeling. Can you feel your feet on the floor? How is your stomach feeling? Put some words to it. Are there places in your body that feel tight or sore? Simply acknowledge them with an "I feel you." Now, notice your breathing. In. Out. In. Out.

Thank You for breath, Jesus. You are my breath.

Thoughts may come knocking now. We are easily distracted and there's so much to do. It can be difficult to quiet our minds. Just notice your thoughts. Acknowledge them. Speak kindly to yourself. "Right. Yes. Don't worry. I'll get back to you in a few minutes."

Notice your breathing again. In. Out.

"He himself gives life and breath to everything." (Acts 17:25 NLT)

"The Spirit of God has made me; the breath of the Almighty gives me life." (Job 33:4)

Jesus, You are my breath. You are my life.
For your next breaths . . . pray this simple prayer as you breathe in and out.

I breathe in Your love, Jesus.
I breathe out Your life.
I breathe in Your love, Jesus.

I breathe out Your life.
I breathe in Your love, Jesus.
I breathe out your life.
I breathe in Your love, Jesus.
I breathe out Your life.

Take deep breaths. Breathe slowly in and out. Continue this gentle prayer for a few more minutes.

And that's it.

Close with these words to Jesus:

Jesus, I worship You as the King of all kings and the Lord of my life. All I am is Yours. You are the very breath I breathe. Thank You for giving me life. You alone are Life! I love You. Thank You for Your love for me. I invite You into every space in my life; into my body, my soul and my spirit. I give myself fully to You. I invite You into all that I need to do today. I invite You into the places I feel apprehensive and concerned. I invite You into the places I feel young and ill equipped. I invite You into the places that I am suffering. Please meet me there. Please help me, Jesus. In the places I don't understand, I ask to trust You. Please help me, dear Jesus, to know You, to love You, and to trust You even more. Thank You that You suffered and died on my behalf. You suffered in ways that I never will. Thank You, Jesus. Thank You.

I invite You in, Jesus. I give You everything. I love You. Thank You for Your immeasurable love for me.

In Jesus' Name,
Amen

SESSION 2

Godly Interference

INTRODUCTION

Group leader reads aloud these opening words from Stasi:

An opportunity came up that allowed me to spend a few days alone on the Oregon coast one spring, and I jumped at it. Late April is still a brown month in Colorado, but in Oregon there were more shades of green than I had words for. I was driving on Highway 101, which curves along the coast, enjoying the large boulders on the seashore that stand like monuments to the glory of God, when the weather suddenly changed. Out of nowhere, the skies opened up with a biblical deluge. Blue skies shifted to dark gray in the blink of an eye. My happy-go-lucky drive turned into one with me crawling down the highway, gripping the steering wheel with my white knuckles.

I hadn't been expecting this.

Now, there's a sentence.

WATCH VIDEO SESSION 2

Video Notes

Use this space to make note of anything that stands out to you in the teaching.

"See what great love the Father has lavished on us, that we should be called children of God. And that is what we are!" (1 John 3:1)

GROUP DISCUSSION: "NEED AND NEEDED"

Gather into small groups if part of a larger group. Spend time together reacting to what Stasi said in the video through these prompts and questions.

Gathering Together

Read aloud as a group the following Scripture:

> "Your word is a lamp for my feet and a light on my path."
> (Psalm 119:105)

Briefly share something you learned from your personal study time.

What jumped out at you or surprised you or struck you most in the video?

Select a volunteer to read the following:

This life we are living is often too difficult to navigate on our own. Which way do we turn? What choice do we make? How do we interpret what is going on? Thankfully, we are not left on our own to figure it out. We have been given the Word of God as a road map, and we have been given the Holy Spirit as our personal Guide. Sometimes things happen as a result of living in a fallen world, and that changes our direction. Sometimes God interferes directly to help us onto the better Way. And sometimes it is both.

In *Defiant Joy*, Stasi shares about how during a workout, she tore her periformis (the little muscle in the glute). Regaining her strength turned into a year-long journey of pain and weakness. The pain had come suddenly, a whiplash-like experience, that hit her out of the blue.

At one time or another—no, many times—we *all* experience situations that come with the force of whiplash.

1. Describe an encounter or life-changing event that struck you with the force of whiplash. What happened?

2. How did you feel afterward?

3. Looking back, can you see where God met you in it?

We are honed both in our needing and in our being needed.

4. Talk about a time when you have been honed for the better by needing others.

Select a volunteer to read this short passage to the group and then discuss the questions that follow:

Not everything that happens to us is the result of God interfering. Often life-altering events are simply the result of living in a fallen world. But at other times, God does interfere directly. In all of it, He uses it for our good—to draw our hearts closer to His.

5. Go around the room and have each woman read this statement, filling in the blank with her own word(s):

    Jesus interferes because He _____.

6. Where has Jesus interfered with you in the past?

7. The "chance" of each of us existing is 1 in 400 billion. And yet, here we are, at such a time as this, because we each have an essential role to play. God will sometimes interfere with our lives so that we might step up higher into our calling. What role would you *love* to play to bring the kingdom of God? How would you like to be used for God's purposes?

Scripture Response

Ask for volunteers to read each of the following verses/passages aloud to the group. Go around the room and have each woman share one word or phrase that comes to mind after hearing these Scriptures:

"May our Lord Jesus Christ himself and God our Father, who loved us and by his grace gave us eternal encouragement and good hope, encourage your hearts and strengthen you in every good deed and word." (2 Thessalonians 2:16–17)

"See what kind of love the Father has given to us, that we should be called children of God; and so we are." (1 John 3:1 ESV)

"I will tell of the LORD's unfailing love.
    I will praise the LORD for all he has done.
I will rejoice in his great goodness to Israel,
    which he has granted according to his mercy and love.
He said, 'They are my very own people.
    Surely they will not betray me again.'
    And he became their Savior.
In all their suffering he also suffered,
    and he personally rescued them.
In his love and mercy he redeemed them.
    He lifted them up and carried them
    through all the years." (Isaiah 63:7–9 NLT)

Leader reads this final note from Stasi:

God is the God of all hope.

He wants us to be a hopeful and joyful people. But we won't be if we base our hope solely on our circumstances or our abilities. Our hope is true and sure only when it is securely fastened to the goodness of our God. And it can be. He wants it to be. We can rest in the truth that we have been pursued and fought for. We have been chosen and set apart. We have a good Father who wants us to know that He is always and ever working for our good. The truth of His love is THE source of encouragement and hope for our lives. We don't have to figure this thing out on our own. We are not alone, and our God wants to strengthen us and bring us encouragement wherever we are. He wants us to know who we are to Him and to rise to the call He has placed on our lives. Ultimately, He wants to share this grand adventure with us.

CLOSING PRAYER

Leader or volunteer, close your group time in prayer:

Dear Father,

I'm so grateful that You are my Father. Thank You that You are committed to growing me up to know You and love You increasingly every day. I need You, God. I need You. Thank You that You are here for me right now. Thank You that You catch me when I fall, You care for me when I'm hurt, and You are always working for my good. You are my good. Please direct my thoughts and my paths, Father. Show me the way I should go. I trust You.

In Jesus' Name,

Amen

Session 2

Personal Study

Read chapters 3–4 in Defiant Joy. *Then, reread the excerpts included here and answer the questions that follow.*

Whiplash goes around. Like a car rear-ending you when you are merely sitting at a stop light waiting patiently for it to change, it strikes you when you least expect it. We are a vulnerable race, us human beings. Even the stronger ones are vulnerable. . . .

We are honed both in our being needed and in our needing. Whether we are the ones experiencing whiplash or the ones walking beside those dealing with the aftereffects, there is joy and growth to be found in the giving and receiving of loving support.

—*Defiant Joy,* pages 42, 44

---

1. In your life, has there been a person who needed you? (Name him or her.) How were you needed? Describe the circumstance or situation and your role.

2. These days, who do *you* need? (Name him or her.) For what? Take your time to really think about it, and write out exactly what you are needing from this person.

Sometimes we can get discouraged when our lives are not going the way we would like them to. We can too easily lose heart when we are weary or vulnerable. *But God.* Two of my favorite words. But God does not look down on us when we are weak. Instead, He loves to come to our aid. He wants to reveal Himself even now as our Strength. He is the God of all Hope.

Read Isaiah 40:28–31:

Do you not know?
    Have you not heard?
The Lord is the everlasting God,
    the Creator of the ends of the earth.
He will not grow tired or weary,
    and his understanding no one can fathom.
He gives strength to the weary
    and increases the power of the weak.
Even youths grow tired and weary,
    and young men stumble and fall;
but those who hope in the Lord
    will renew their strength.
They will soar on wings like eagles;
    they will run and not grow weary,
    they will walk and not be faint.

3. Is there an area in your life that you need God to come and increase your strength spiritually, physically, emotionally, or relationally? Where? Write it here and turn it into a prayer.

A daughter of the King is worth caring for.

4. God cares for you. You are a priority to Him. I wrote in *Defiant Joy* that self-care is an area I too easily let slip. Would you say that you are good at self-care? What care are you needing these days?

Who you are flows from WHOSE you are.

5. Our identity is the basis for our every thought and every action. Put some words to this truth and claim it for yourself here. What does this truth mean to you?

6. Look up Colossians 3:12. Write three adjectives that this verse uses to describe you.

• _____

• _____

• _____

It is from a place of intimacy with Jesus that we learn: We can offer life because we're accepted. We don't offer in order to gain acceptance. We have a purpose because we're called. We don't have it in order to become called. We are a child of God because the Father has chosen us. We are not a child because we somehow wormed our way into His heart by our actions. We are pursued by Jesus not because we are amazing but because He is.

Our identity is always under assault. I need to know who I am as His beloved daughter so I can stand against the enemy's assault and silence the voice of the accuser. So do you.

We all ache for a Father.

I want to know God as my good Father who is constantly intervening on my behalf. I want to know my Jesus and the Holy Spirit who are constantly interfering with my ways that inhibit me from living as a daughter of God so I can step into the fullness of what He has for me and, through me, for the world.

—Stasi

7. What do you want? What do you want to do? Be specific and be honest.

8. What's held you back?

9. Who do you feel *God* calling you to be? Describe here.

Because we are instructed to: *(summarize Hebrews 12:1)*

And promised that: *(summarize Isaiah 40:31)*

We can declare: *(write down Psalm 119:32)*

How do we get there? How do we run free? How do we offer without fear? We respond to the love of God by choosing to believe it. We rest in His love even when we feel we are failing. We press into it when we feel unworthy. We open our hands that are clenched in fear-filled control and yield in trust to His good heart. We don't resist God's interference with our lives but instead pray to recognize it and pursue Him in it. We spend time in God's Word when we want to, but especially when we don't.

And we carve out times in our calendars for opportunities to encounter His love, hear His voice, and receive the blessing of growing in knowing our God intimately.

I love the story of a certain man whom Jesus interfered with, much to his initial chagrin. Remember when Jesus met the man possessed with many demons in Luke 8?

So they arrived in the region of the Gerasenes, across the lake from Galilee. As Jesus was climbing out of the boat, a man who was possessed by demons came out to meet him. For a long time he had been homeless and naked, living in the tombs outside the town. As soon as he saw Jesus, he shrieked and fell down in front of him. Then he screamed, "Why are you interfering with me, Jesus, Son of the Most High God?" (vv. 26–28 NLT)

The man in this true story was tormented by demons to the point that it was impossible for him to live a healthy life. He was isolated from his family and friends, not able to work or do anything other than endure the excruciating torment.

And after many years of this, Jesus showed up. When He did, the man came running naked to Him (that must have been a little unnerving—at least for the disciples), shouting, "What are You doing here? Why are You interfering with me? This is my life. I'm fine. Leave me alone!"

Huh. We all know he wasn't fine. His life had not been his own for quite some time. In fact, it wasn't him at all who was shouting at Jesus to go away but the inner tormenting demons compelled by fear. And Jesus, mighty Love incarnate, refused to leave. Instead He interfered; He intervened.

Jesus crossed the Sea of Galilee, all sixty-four square miles, to get to this one man. And He has crossed galaxies and heavenly realms to get to you. He passed through unimaginable opposition and endured unfathomable suffering to get to you. To mess with you. He has come, and He is coming still. To save us. To heal us. To help us. To love us. To guide and comfort us. And to interfere with our lives—particularly in the places we do not want Him to.

Yes, it can be uncomfortable, but remember who Jesus is. He has the right to interfere.

—*Defiant Joy*, pages 56–57

10. Where has Jesus interfered with you in the past?

Sometimes the conviction of the Holy Spirit feels like interference. It is. Jesus is standing in our way to show us a better way. To show us His Way.

11. Do you feel him interfering with you these days? Said another way, do you sense him calling you to live differently—perhaps in a relationship, at work, or in your private moments alone? Where?

The man possessed by Legion asked Jesus, "Why are you interfering with me?" You know the answer. It's the same one He has for you. Because He loves him. And He loves you.

So, again, why do think He interferes with you? He interferes with you because He wants you to know who you are.

All life, all identity, all purpose flow from our connection with the Father.

Who are you? You are a child of the living God. You were chosen before the foundations of the earth to be holy. You are loved beyond telling. You are the beloved of Jesus, the bride of Christ. You are the beauty of the kingdom. You are Christ's ambassador. You are bringing the kingdom of God with you wherever you go. And you are hated. By one that Jesus has conquered, defeated, and disarmed—and you have authority over him.

As children of the living God, we are no longer defined by our pasts, our wounds, or our sins. We are not defined by our failures but by the finished work of Christ.

> You are a daughter first, a beloved child of the Creator of creation, the Lord of heaven and earth from whom every good gift flows. We need to know the truth and marinate our hearts in the Scripture—of both who our God is and who we are because of all that Jesus won for us—in order to stand our ground in UNWAVERING DEFIANCE against the world's tides that would like to sweep us away into a false sense of self.
>
> You belong to God. You are not your own. Jesus has the right to interfere with your life. We can know that any and all interference that He chooses to set in our way is for our good. He interferes because He loves us.
>
> —Stasi

12. Look up 1 John 3:1 and write it here.

13. Read Ephesians 2:10 and summarize it in your own words.

The New Living Translation of Ephesians 2:10 says, "For we are God's masterpiece." This may sound far-fetched today, but take a few moments right now and *consider the possibility that it is true.* You are the pinnacle of creation. Most days, we don't feel like that. Whether you do or don't, take a moment and thank God that He sees you as His masterpiece.

14. Read 2 Corinthians 5:20. What is one of your roles as a believer?

You are here—now—at such a time as this because you have a vital role to play to bring His kingdom. Jesus is messing with you because He wants to heal and transform you. He is interfering with you because He needs you to know that you are first and last your Father's beloved daughter. He wants you to know who you are and to step up into all that means.

Jesus came and He is coming again, and when He does, He will INTERFERE WITH EVERYTHING and make all things right, all things new, including you and me. Now that's a reason for unwavering joy!

St. Patrick's Breastplate

I arise today
Through a mighty strength, the invocation of the Trinity,
Through belief in the Threeness,
Through confession of the Oneness
of the Creator of creation.

I arise today
Through the strength of Christ's birth with His baptism,
Through the strength of His crucifixion with His burial,
Through the strength of His resurrection with His ascension,
Through the strength of His descent for the judgment of doom.

I arise today
Through the strength of the love of cherubim,
In the obedience of angels,
In the service of archangels,
In the hope of resurrection to meet with reward,

In the prayers of patriarchs,
In the predictions of prophets,
In the preaching of apostles,
In the faith of confessors,
In the innocence of holy virgins,
In the deeds of righteous men.

I arise today, through
The strength of heaven,
The light of the sun,
The radiance of the moon,
The splendor of fire,
The speed of lightning,
The swiftness of wind,
The depth of the sea,
The stability of the earth,
The firmness of rock.

I arise today, through
God's strength to pilot me,
God's might to uphold me,
God's wisdom to guide me,
God's eye to look before me,
God's ear to hear me,
God's word to speak for me,
God's hand to guard me,
God's shield to protect me,
God's host to save me
From snares of devils,
From temptation of vices,
From everyone who shall wish me ill,
afar and near.

I summon today
All these powers between me and those evils,
Against every cruel and merciless power
that may oppose my body and soul,
Against incantations of false prophets,
Against black laws of pagandom,
Against false laws of heretics,
Against craft of idolatry,
Against spells of witches and smiths and wizards,
Against every knowledge that corrupts man's body and soul;
Christ to shield me today
Against poison, against burning,
Against drowning, against wounding,
So that there may come to me an abundance of reward.

Christ with me,
Christ before me,
Christ behind me,
Christ in me,
Christ beneath me,
Christ above me,
Christ on my right,
Christ on my left,
Christ when I lie down,
Christ when I sit down,
Christ when I arise,
Christ in the heart of every man who thinks of me,
Christ in the mouth of everyone who speaks of me,
Christ in every eye that sees me,
Christ in every ear that hears me.

WORSHIP SONG

Pick any one of them—or all of them! Put it (them) on repeat! Find a time to listen when you are not distracted by many other things. Bless you.

- "Reckless Love" – Cory Asbury
- "Find Me" – Jonathan David and Melissa Helser
- "Where You Are" – Leeland

CONTEMPLATIVE PRAYER

This week, set aside five to ten minutes in a quiet and comfortable place.

Begin by praying:

Holy Spirit, I pray You would guide me into understanding how the story in Luke about the man possessed by demons applies to me. I am not a demon-possessed man living among the tombs, yet I know that You have moved mountains to come and rescue me. Where do I need rescuing today? Is it in a negative relationship? Is it in a commitment to self-protection that keeps me from being honest with myself and You? Show me, Lord. I sanctify my imagination to You, Lord. Come for me, Jesus. Come now, please.

Reread Luke 8:26–28.

Take a few deep, settling breaths.

Imagine yourself in this man's place. Picture yourself standing alone and you see Jesus walking toward you. He is walking to you with loving intent. As He gets closer, you can see the kindness in His eyes. You know that He has come just for you. You know that He has come because He loves you.

Imagine asking Him, "Where do You want to interfere with me, Lord?"

Sit with this for a while. This isn't a time to soul-search but just to allow God to surface a place in your heart or your life where you need to know and trust His love more deeply.

Pray to invite Him in, to yield to Him, to receive His love in this very place. Thank Him for His gentle and persistent pursuit.

Greener Grass

INTRODUCTION

Group leader reads aloud these opening words from Stasi:

Sometimes I want to run away from my life. The problem lies in two areas when I do run away. First and most obviously, I come along with myself and my "self" is actually what I am trying to get away from. And second, if I am successful at running away, even to a movie for a couple of hours, everything I left behind is waiting for me as soon as I come back.

When I want to escape, often the cry rising from my heart is, "I want to go home." I didn't know what that cry meant for many years. If I was in the grocery store and the feeling was extremely strong, I would leave my shopping and go home. Later, while "home," I had the same longing. Finally, I realized I was longing for my True Home.

My True Home that I will dwell in forever is coming. But my True Home doesn't have to wait. My home is in God. He is my Home. When I come home to Him in my heart, my anxiousness and fear fade away. They melt into His welcoming arms. The only running I want to do is straight to Him.

WATCH VIDEO SESSION 3

Video Notes

Use this space to make note of anything that stands out to you in the teaching.

" . . . to bestow on them a crown of beauty instead of ashes, the oil of joy instead of mourning, and a garment of praise instead of a spirit of despair." (Isaiah 61:3)

GROUP DISCUSSION: "GREENER GRASS"

Gather into small groups if part of a larger group. Spend time together reacting to what Stasi said in the video through these prompts and questions.

Gathering Together

Read aloud as a group the following Scripture:

> "For you did not receive a spirit that makes you a slave again to fear, but you received the Spirit of sonship. And by him we cry, 'Abba, Father.'" (Romans 8:15 NIV 1984)

Briefly share something you learned from your personal study time.

What jumped out at you or surprised you or struck you most in the video?

1. When you were a little girl seeking "greener grass" in your life when your world became too brown, where did you go?

2. Do you have times now when you would like to run away from your life? Where do you go? What are you hoping to find?

3. In your life, where can you see that God has pursued you?

4. Stasi tells the story of having the joy of going to Israel and standing outside of Lazarus's tomb. God called her to: "Come out." "Come alive." Where is one place in you that God is calling you to "come out" from? Where do you feel God is calling you to "come alive"?

5. In the midst of a dire diagnosis, Stasi's friend Craig said, "I have many reasons to grieve; I have many more to worship." Take turns sharing some reasons you have to worship.

Scripture Response

Ask for volunteers to read each of the following verses/passages aloud to the group. Go around the room and have each woman share one word or phrase that comes to mind after hearing these Scriptures:

"Where can I go from your Spirit?
     Where can I flee from your presence?
If I go up to the heavens, you are there;
     if I make my bed in the depths, you are there.
If I rise on the wings of the dawn,
     if I settle on the far side of the sea,
even there your hand will guide me,
     your right hand will hold me fast." (Psalm 139:7–10)

"There is a time for everything,
     and a season for every activity under the heavens . . .
a time to weep and a time to laugh,
     a time to mourn and a time to dance." (Ecclesiastes 3:1, 4)

"Truly, truly, I say to you, whoever hears my word and believes him who sent me has eternal life. He does not come into judgment, but has passed from death to life." (John 5:24 ESV)

Leader reads this final note from Stasi:

One of the ways we tend our hearts is to tell our story and honor what we have lived. It is a worthy and good thing to do with a safe person or a group where a covenant of confidentially and a culture of honor are in place. If you have not experienced that yet, pray that you will.

CLOSING PRAYER

Leader or volunteer, close your group time in prayer:

Dearest Father,

There are times and places in my life where I have run. Running was sometimes the best option. But now, the only running I want to do is straight into Your arms. To do that, I need to know You as my good Father. I know in my head that You are. I pray to know it more deeply in my heart. Would You please show me how You have been pursuing me all my life? I know that You proved Your love for me once and for all when You gave Your Son to die on my behalf. He paid the price I could never pay. Thank You, Abba. Thank You. I worship You. I need You. I run to You. You have done all that was required. You are My enough—You are enough for me. Still, would You please reveal Your love to me once again. I know it's something You love to do.

I love you.

In Jesus' Name,

Amen

Session 3

Personal Study

Read chapters 5–6 in Defiant Joy. *Then, reread the excerpts included here and answer the questions that follow.*

> Have you ever gone looking for a reprieve, for a taste of beauty, for a respite, for an escape when your world became too complicated or too overwhelming or just too brown? Did you think everything might be better somewhere else, anywhere else? Maybe you were a little girl who went to the swing set or the tree fort. Maybe you went to your grandmother's house or walked in a field. As a young woman, did you try to run somewhere that felt safer when life became too threatening? Where did you go? To a book? To a movie? To a man? To church?
>
> Were you a [child] who, searching for greener grass, escaped into the wild of the backyard or the Amazonian ditch behind your home? . . . did you go to magazines, to music, to sports, to books, [to food,] not knowing you were searching for a way to soothe your soul? Or maybe you did know.
>
> —*Defiant Joy*, pages 69–70

1. If you could run away right now, to where would it be? What is appealing to you about that place? *the beach where it's warm. the water*

The world does become too complicated, too overwhelming, too filled with pain so much of the time. As children, we don't have the capacity to make sense of it, let alone process it. If our lives become too filled with trauma, a part of us disappears. We push down what we can't understand or resolve and instead go looking for greener grass to distract us from the ache. But that doesn't really work. At least not in the long-term.

[As adults,] we need to stop our running. We need to tend our hearts. One of the best ways we can do that is by honoring the story of our lives, by letting that part of us and our past that has been tamped down rise back to the surface, and then inviting Jesus into it. If we are to find our way to an authentic life characterized by joy, one that isn't constantly looking for something better elsewhere, we will need to face the truth about our lives with merciful honesty and choose to linger in it long enough for the Holy Spirit to do His gentle yet persistent redemptive work.

—*Defiant Joy*, page 70

*   *   *

Your life is a story. It's a story of how your heart was handled—it's a story of how God has pursued you and how the enemy has assaulted you.

And for all of us, that pursuit and that assault began when we were very young.

—Stasi

2. Looking back, describe where you have seen God pursue you. (Remember, God's pursuit can be in something that you loved.)

3. Wounds come to us beginning at an early age. We live in a fallen and broken world. Often those wounds shape how we feel about ourselves. Are you aware of a defining wound you received early in your life? What is it? When did it occur? Be gentle with yourself here. This is holy ground.

4. How do you feel about yourself on a good day?

5. How about on one that's not so great? Can you remember when that message of you being not quite good enough was first delivered to you?

6. Invite Jesus in to speak the (truth) to you in that very place. What does He think?
    What does He say?

7. Look up the following Scriptures and write down a word or two about how God
    sees you and feels about you.

    Isaiah 43:4   precious , honored, He loves us

    Song of Songs 4:1   beautiful beyond words

    Colossians 3:12   holy , dearly loved, God's chosen

    Ephesians 5:1   dear children , followers of God

    We are all meant to be loved intentionally and powerfully by our fathers. My father
failed me, but I have come to know that the deepest reality is that he loved me. Looking
back, I see many times when he showed his love for me.

8. Do you have memories of your father loving you? What is one?

9. If you do or you don't, what does that stir in you?

None of us had a perfect father. That man does not exist. The ache we feel in the place our father was meant to speak life, but didn't, can leave a lasting mark. But we have a God who has come to heal our broken hearts. He wants to do that.

[I want to tell you the truth and I want you to hear it!] You *have* a good, good father. [God is your Father.] He *is* Father. It's not merely what He does; it's who He is. You don't have to pack your bag and run away, searching for a better one. You already have the best one. Your Father is the One who has been pursuing you, protecting you, and loving you your entire life.

God, your Father, is love. He loved you as a child, and He loves you now. Right now.

—*Defiant Joy*, page 79

---

10. Where in your heart, in your life do you need Him to redeem the word *father* for you?   *Building me up*
    Acceptance
    Love

11. In what ways do you need Him to redeem your story for you?

12. Do you want to know God as Father? If so, ask Him. He would love to come for you. Write a prayer from your heart asking Him to come for yours.

Because You are loved. Right now. When God looks at you, He sees the one for whom He gave everything and won everything so that you could be with Him forever. You are chosen. You are the apple of His eye. You are the joy that was set before Jesus. Ask God to help you know that. Ask for His view on your life.

There is a time to ask. It is now.

> The larger story, the gospel, reminds us that we live in a fallen world and sin abounds. We know that we have an enemy and he is loose, roaming the earth, searching for those he can devour, shred, and maul. He works through fallen people, even through broken, imperfect Christians, to steal, kill, and destroy. And God loves those people. Not the harm they cause—but the Father loves them (and us) so much that He sent His Son to die for all of us. He is for you. He fights for you. He woos you. He protects you from further unimaginable harm that you will never endure and even in the worst of pain, He is fierce on your behalf.

You can rest in His love. The end of your story is a good one. The grass we will walk in one day when Jesus returns is lush and thick and fragrant.

—Defiant Joy, page 81

* * *

I had the privilege of visiting Jerusalem a few years ago—being in those places where David once danced. It was an incredible experience to go to places I had read of and wondered at for so long. One day, I was awed to be standing outside of Lazarus's tomb. While there, the pastor leading our little group asked us to inquire of God if there were places within us that we had closed in a grave. I knew the answer for me was yes. I was tired. I was hurting. Betrayal from a friend had left me wanting to shrink back from all people. My passion for life had dimmed. My zeal to tell others of the wonders of Jesus had faded. I realized a part of my heart had become buried. And then I felt His call. ["COME OUT!"]

Jesus' call to us is the same as His call to Lazarus as He stood before His grave in John 11: "Come out!" he commanded. "Come alive!" We are not meant to live in a tomb. Our callings are needed in the world; they are not to be buried under the burden of others' demands or judgments. Pain comes, but it does not get to seal our graves.

—Defiant Joy, page 88

13. So I ask you, where is death for you? What song has died on your lips at the critics' continual shaming of your voice?

In that very place, Jesus commands you loudly and firmly to "come out." And He says it with tears. With mercy. He is fierce in His instruction and in His intercession for you. He has life for you. Life. Ask Jesus where the tomb holds you and then answer His call.

Jesus has intervened on our behalf that we might make divine exchanges. From death to life. From addiction to freedom. From heartbreak to hope.

14. The Scriptures make it clear that nothing is impossible for God. Thank goodness. What feels impossible for you?

15. One of the divine exchanges is from fear to trust. Where has fear gripped you in the past or is holding you now?

16. What would trusting Jesus in this place look like for you?

turning it over to God

17. What divine exchange would you like to make?

*uncertainty to certainty in the
H. Spirit
my thoughts for His thoughts & guidance*

Ecclesiastes 3 says, "There is a time for everything, and a season for every activity under the heavens . . . a time to weep and a time to laugh, a time to mourn and a time to dance" (vv. 1, 4).

Let's make the divine exchange. Stop our running *away from* and begin running *to* our good Father. Let's exchange death for life. Let's receive what our Father has promised us.

" . . . to bestow on them a crown of beauty instead of ashes, the oil of joy instead of mourning, and a garment of praise instead of a spirit of despair." (Isaiah 61:3)

WORSHIP SONG

Pick any one of them—or all of them! Put it (them) on repeat! Find a time to listen when you are not distracted by many other things. Bless you.

- Lean Back – Capital City Music
- My Home Is You – Darrell Evans
- You Came (Lazarus) – Jonathan David and Melissa Helser

CONTEMPLATIVE PRAYER

Begin by setting aside at least five minutes (ten would be even better) to sit quietly in the Presence of God.

Pray:

I consecrate this time to You, God. I give it to You. I yield to You my expectations and desires and ask You to come for me again. I give You all of me and I sanctify the gift of my imagination to You. I pray to hear Your voice.

Take a few deep breaths to get comfortable and settle yourself.

Picture yourself standing outside of Lazarus's tomb or perhaps even inside it. You can hear Jesus calling with a tender fierceness, "Come out!"

Then Jesus shouted, "Lazarus, come out!" (John 11:43)

He is calling you to come out from places you have shrunk back from or tried to bury. "Come out," He calls again.

You answer, "Here I am, Lord."

Talk to Jesus about where you feel buried. Invite Him to meet you in that very place. Imagine yourself taking His hand and walking out. What does He say to your heart?

Ask Him to help you exchange death for life. Ask Him to heal your hurting heart. It's what He came to do.

Expectant Hope

INTRODUCTION

Group leader reads aloud these opening words from Stasi:

God loves to speak to His children. He is the Word. He speaks to us all the time through it, through His creation, through other people, and through the still small voice in our hearts where He dwells. He is endlessly creative in how He speaks to us, as He has the entire universe at His disposal and under His command. Through it all, the primary message He is trying to get across is *"I love you."*

He also likes to speak to us in and about our current circumstances. At the beginning of each year, my husband John and I ask God for a word over the year—a canopy under which He would specifically like us to live. My word over this year is *believe*. It's a good word to have, as it is by and in faith that we please God—and I want to please Him. By faith, we each can ask to hear His voice and press in to hear Him more clearly.

WATCH VIDEO SESSION 4

Video Notes

Use this space to make note of anything that stands out to you in the teaching.

"Blessed is she who has believed that the Lord would fulfill what he promised to her!" (Luke 1:45)

GROUP DISCUSSION: "WAITING"

Gather into small groups if part of a larger group. Spend time together reacting to what Stasi said in the video through these prompts and questions.

Gathering Together

Read aloud as a group the following Scripture:

> "May the God of hope fill you with all joy and peace as you trust in him, so that you may overflow with hope by the power of the Holy Spirit." (Romans 15:13)

Briefly share something you learned from your personal study time.

What jumped out at you or surprised you or struck you most in the video?

1. What are you waiting *for?* Go around the room and have each woman name one or two things she is waiting for.

2. What are you waiting *in*? Go around the room again and have each woman name what she is waiting in—the context or environment of her waiting. (Ex.: pain and suffering, fear, family history, circumstances)

3. Waiting requires trust that your waiting will not be in vain. Discuss the vulnerability of waiting. Does it make you feel exposed or secure? Does it inspire confidence or doubt?

4. What is your personal, silent hope? Take a few moments to get quiet with the Lord and be honest with Him. Let your hope rise up from the depths and pour out of you. What is your hope? Share it with the group if you are comfortable; otherwise just write it here and let yourself see your hope live on the page.

5. What has God promised you? Be specific. Share something either recently or in your past that you feel God has promised you. Discuss whether or not that promise has been fulfilled yet. How does it feel or did it feel to wait for the promise to be fulfilled?

6. God made some outrageous promises to David, anointing him as the next king of Israel. God is always faithful to keep His promises, and David knew that. Still, for many years, David found himself not the king, but the hunted.

   Share with the group if you have ever felt like you, too, were living in a cave, not knowing the outcome? What does that dark place of unknowing feel like?

7. Stasi said she prays, "I give everyone and everything to you, God." How easy or difficult is that to pray when you are waiting? Why?

8. Why do you think joy is so difficult to know while we wait on God's promise? Do you find yourself experiencing joy and hope at the same time? Name and share one way you will approach waiting with joy and knowing joy in your hope.

Leader reads these words from Stasi:

I want to encourage you to ask God for a word or a Scripture from Him over this current season. Simply ask Him . . . and wait with an expectant and attentive heart.

Scripture Response

Ask for volunteers to read each of the following verses/passages aloud to the group. Go around the room and have each woman share one word or phrase that comes to mind after hearing these Scriptures:

> "The Lord is not slow to fulfill his promise as some count slowness, but is patient toward you, not wishing that any should perish, but that all should reach repentance." (2 Peter 3:9 ESV)

> "Be anxious for nothing . . . and the peace of God . . . will guard your hearts and minds in Christ Jesus." (Philippians 4:6–7 NASB)

> "Rejoice in hope, be patient in tribulation, be constant in prayer." (Romans 12:12 ESV)

CLOSING PRAYER

Leader or volunteer, close your group time in prayer:

Dear God, You know all things. You know what I am waiting for. I pray that You would deepen my trust in You and my hope in Your promises to me. I proclaim that as I wait, You are forging gold in my heart. You wait with me. Father, I look to You. I believe You are good. And I pray that You would fill me with joy and peace as I trust You and that I would overflow with hope by the power of the Holy Spirit.

In Jesus' Name I pray,

Amen

Session 4

Personal Study

Read chapters 7–8 in Defiant Joy. *Then, answer the questions that follow.*

> **Have you ever asked God for a word over your year? Ask Him now and write His answer—His word over your year—right here:**

1. As discussed in the video, David hid in the caves of Adullam for four years. Had God abandoned him? How do you know?

2. Look up 1 Corinthians 1:9. Write it here.

3. Describe where you have seen God's faithfulness in your life in the past.

We also know that David knew God did not abandon him there in the darkness because David was a worshipper. It was in the caves that he wrote Psalm 57:

> Be exalted, O God, above the heavens;
>> let your glory be over all the earth. . . .
> For great is your love, reaching to the heavens;
>> your faithfulness reaches to the skies. (Psalm 57:5, 10)

4. In those years of hiding, God was forming the greatest king Israel had ever known. In your places of waiting for God's promises to be fulfilled for you, what might He be forging in you?

5. Look up and write down Hebrews 11:23.

6. Read the following verses and write the promise they each describe:

    Hebrews 13:5

    Isaiah 41:10

James 4:7

1 John 1:9

Deuteronomy 31:8

*Possessing a defiant and unwavering joy does
not mean we won't be sad sometimes.*

God calls us even in the sad, or dark, or hard places to awaken to the hope we have in Christ. He does not despise our sadness but desires to meet with us in it. When we do that, our sadness can bear the fruit of helping us awaken to the longings in our hearts. Even in the midst of sadness, we can know a defiant joy.

Living with defiant joy is not easy. Defiant joy is opposed. Perhaps that should be the title of this book. We all know this opposition keenly. Choosing joy can feel like pushing a massive boulder up a steep hill, impossible without the help of others. But if we were not meant to walk in and know joy intimately, why would God have commanded that we do? We are prodded, invited, and instructed to have joy even in the face of loss, suffering, and pain. In many ways, it's a call to live in the realm of the miraculous. Of course, following this call, along with every other move toward the life God wants for us, means we will be opposed.

And behind all opposition, there is one who opposes. Behind all thieveries, there is a thief. Remember what Jesus said in John 10:10: "The thief comes only to steal and kill and destroy." Satan comes to rob us of our joy, our peace, and our connection to and faith in God. He whispers lies to us when we are vulnerable and does his best to warp our perception of our lives with his depressing and evil spin. His endless attacks can wear a person down if they aren't aware that the perceptions being suggested are coming straight from hell.

Satan is very good at stealing. He's devoted all of his malice to separating us from intimacy with our good Father and the experience of deep joy that comes straight from Jesus' heart. The evil one uses the circumstances of our lives and of the world to bring discouragement and despair. That is why we must remember that, though happiness is rooted in our circumstances, joy is rooted in eternity.

We were born into a world at war. It manifests itself in a variety of ways, but all of them come against our union with God. All of them steal our joy. We are not to live in fear of the war, but we are to be armed and shielded in the power of God, living with wisdom and awareness in it.

Our hearts need to be grounded in the unchanging truth of the love of God so that the manifold thieves that come our way do not have their way. To press on to the life Jesus has won for us and calls us to, we need to be aware of the enemy's schemes. We need to remember—even when we are weighted down by the worries, demands, and pressures of life, even when we feel that we are failing in them—that the Father invites us to rest in His arms and find reassurance in His heart toward us. His heart is the only safe place for ours.

—*Defiant Joy*, pages 121–123

7. From what opposition are you longing to be released?

Poison & Cure

Worry

What are you tempted to worry about?
The antidote is faith and prayer.

Accusation

Where are you feeling accused?
The antidote is the blood of Christ.

Fear

Where has fear taken hold in your heart, in your mind, in your life?
The antidote is the Spirit of love, power, and a sound mind.

Pressure

What do you feel weighted down by?
The antidote is the strength of Christ within you.

Comparison

In what ways are you comparing yourself to others in ways that bring
discouragement?
*The antidote is to fix your gaze on Jesus alone. Ask His perspective on you and
your life.*

Resentment

Where are you holding on to regret or resentment over a situation in your life?
Name it.
The antidote is forgiveness.

Benevolent detachment on behalf of others is more than just a theory. It's an imperative. Yes, we should care. But we cannot fully carry. Only God can do that. And He loves to carry, to rescue, and to intervene. We may be weak and inadequate to carry the load, but when we turn to Jesus and give it to Him, He reveals His strength to those we care for.

I am learning that when I feel like a person's well-being is completely up to me, then I have taken on more than is mine to carry. There are times when I am meant to intervene on a person's behalf, and there are times when I am meant to walk alongside someone in caring support. I love those times. But the need for boundaries is real for all of us, and we will never be able to establish them within our own souls if we feel the pressure to come through for someone beyond what God intends. When we are weighed down by the pressure to come through on another's behalf, joy flies out the window.

I tend to believe that people are my sole responsibility to help, but then I remember God. I remember that He is good. I remember that He is a God who intervenes. He is the God of all hope. He restores what is lost. He can care for my friend. He can turn this around. He is always moving on our and others' behalf, much more than we can see in any given moment. He is much more capable than I am. Yes, I want to partner with Him in bringing healing and life, but I need to follow His lead.

So I pray for and then release my friend to God. I remember that I am not the one responsible for her; God is. Though I love her, my becoming worried and depressed on her behalf is not going to help. Truly loving her means I must detach my soul and allow my hope for her to rise. My joy cannot be rooted in any other person's well-being, and my possessing deep joy in the midst of another's pain does not diminish her sorrow nor my love for her. I am meant to trust God deeply and trust Him with all my cares. Even my care for those closest to me. Benevolent detachment breeds the possibility of joy.

—*Defiant Joy*, pages 124–125

8. Put the concept of benevolent detachment into your own words.

Practicing benevolent detachment is not an unloving thing to do but actually a deeply loving action. It helps us get out of God's way so that He is freer to intervene.

9. Is there someone (or many persons) that you need to lovingly extricate yourself from and practice benevolent detachment with? Name the person(s) or the situation(s).

10. After reading the verses you looked up in question 6 and considering the faithfulness of God, describe how you can wait with hope for the fulfillment of His promises to you.

11. As Luke 1:45 says of Mary, "Blessed is she who has believed that the Lord would fulfill his promises to her!" What promise do you want to believe Him for?

WORSHIP SONG

Pick any one of them—or all of them! Put it (them) on repeat! Find a time to listen when you are not distracted by many other things. Bless you.

- "Worth the Wait" – Bryan McCleery
- "Take Courage" – Kristene DiMarco (Bethel Music)
- "You Are All I Need" – Dara Maclean

CONTEMPLATIVE PRAYER

"May the God of hope fill you with all joy and peace, as you trust in him, so that you may overflow with hope by the power of the Holy Spirit." (Romans 15:13)

Quiet yourself.

Take a few deep breaths to help to calm and center yourself.

Say the above verse aloud to yourself slowly, twice.

Write a prayer of your own declaring your belief in God's promises and the hope that you have because of them. Be specific.

Now, read it aloud to Him.

SESSION 5

Cultivating Joy

INTRODUCTION

Group leader reads aloud these opening words from Stasi:

A season ends. The freedom of childhood has been replaced with the responsibilities of adulthood. Later, the children have moved out or the possibility of having children has moved on. The vacation is over and whether it was close to what one hoped for or nothing near it, the dream of it has vanished. The job we held has shut its doors to us. The relationships we took for granted have changed and whether we know why or not, the world has once again shifted.

Our next breath, our next thought, our next emotion turns on a belief, one we hold as tightly to our chest as a professional poker player. We may not even know what is in our hand. We may not be able to speak it, but we will reveal it. Our beliefs will unfold through a look in our eyes. Is it a hungry one, a belief being petted and nursed on a steady diet of fear and doubt, reinforced by a rehearsal of past pain? Is it a curious look? A look in the eye that evokes a question?

Is it a resigned one?

Or is the look that is in the eye a settled, restful one?

The woman in Proverbs 31, held up as a model of godliness, often strikes us as a woman of unattainable stature. Who is this woman who laughs at the future? Friend, she does not laugh to mock it or to challenge it. She laughs at it because she is not afraid of it. And she is not afraid of it because she knows her God holds it; He holds her and He holds all she cares for.

We can know that as well.

There is a great good coming in the future to us. Always. Always. No matter what.

WATCH VIDEO SESSION 5

Video Notes

Use this space to make note of anything that stands out to you in the teaching.

"So also you have sorrow now, but I will see you again, and your hearts will rejoice, and no one will take your joy from you." (John 16:22 ESV)

GROUP DISCUSSION: "SIGNS AND MEANINGS"

Gather into small groups if part of a larger group. Spend time together reacting to what Stasi said in the video through these prompts and questions.

Gathering Together

Read aloud as a group the following Scripture:

> "She is clothed with strength and dignity; she can laugh at the days to come." (Proverbs 31:25)

Briefly share something you learned from your personal study time.

What jumped out at you or surprised you or struck you most in the video?

1. What is your favorite season? Why? Does it lead you to thinking forward or to reflecting back?

2. God gives many signs: signs in nature; through longing and beauty; through pain, celebrations, and endings; and primarily in His Word. What do the signs point to? As a group, make a list of signs God gives us and discuss the similarities and differences in what different signs point to.

3. Think for a moment about endings, especially how they make you feel. Have you ever had sorrow at an ending? How about joy? Consider one specific ending—joyful or sorrowful—and share how that ending felt and why if you are comfortable.

4. Now think for moment about beginnings. In what ways do beginnings feel differently and similarly to endings? Discuss how beginnings can feel so hopeful and endings so full of sorrow, yet our ultimate ending is full of all hope.

5. What is something you are looking forward to in this next season of life?

6. How would you describe your ultimate future? What has God promised you?

7. What is one of the first things you would love to do when you arrive in heaven? Why?

8. As gratitude is the key that unlocks joy, what are a few things that you can be grateful for today?

Scripture Response

Ask for volunteers to read each of the following verses/passages aloud to the group. Go around the room and have each woman share one word or phrase that comes to mind after hearing these Scriptures:

> "So Jesus said to him, 'Unless you see signs and wonders you will not believe.'" (John 4:48 ESV)

"Tell us, when will these things happen? And what will be the sign that they are all about to be fulfilled?" (Mark 13:4)

"But thanks be to God! He gives us the victory through our Lord Jesus Christ. Therefore, my dear brothers and sisters, stand firm. Let nothing move you. Always give yourselves fully to the work of the Lord, because you know that your labor in the Lord is not in vain." (1 Corinthians 15:57-58)

CLOSING PRAYER

Leader or volunteer, close your group time in prayer:

Dearest Jesus,

I am so grateful for the victory that You have won over death. Because of Your unending life, I too have unending Life in You. Praise You. God, open my eyes to see the signs around me every day that point to the truth of Your resurrection and the life that is coming to me one day. Help me to remember the ways that You have come to me in my past. You are faithful. I confess that as You have been faithful to me in the past, so You will be faithful to me in the future. I can look to the future with a restful heart. I am so very thankful for that. Truly.

In Your Name I pray,

Amen

Session 5

Personal Study

Read chapters 9–10 in Defiant Joy. *Then, reread the excerpts included here and answer the questions that follow.*

Gentle invitations surround us that point us to the truth of the goodness and promises of God.

Scrub oak covers the hills in the Front Range of Colorado. They are the last to leaf out, stubborn in their arrival come summer, and the first to fall in the blustery wind that signals its end. But, oh, they are marvelous. The soft virgin lime-green leaves that bud first are velvet to the touch. After so long a season of bareness, seeing them emerge causes my breath to catch in my throat. Then suddenly, when I'm not looking, they fill out, exploding with green. They soak up the sun with their abundant life and cover the hills like a carpet of emeralds. The canopy of deep summer is their lively playground. They provide cover for the spotted and gangly newborn fawns and a nesting place for the hummingbirds, who make their home in its lush leaves as soon as they arrive.

Then comes a shift in the wind, a hint on the breeze, a coolness I feel but am not ready to admit to, and the leaves of the scrub oak begin to turn. First a slight hint of gold around the edges warns that, like nomads, the leaves will not stay long. Oranges and reds engulf the green next like hungry flames. It is the scrub oak's stunning swan song. An autumn patchwork replaces the solid sea of jade, and I know the quilt will not linger. In the Rocky Mountains, autumn falls as quickly from the landscape as a shooting star.

The wind blows harder. The leaves come down, dry now and brown, littering the landscape with their final goodbye.

The branches are naked then. The view through them no longer blocked. When the snow falls softly, it lands on the branches gently, dusting one side with powdered-sugar grace. On very cold days, they become embroidered with icy crystal lace. But, mostly, they are naked. Brown. Empty. It takes an effort to see the beauty that remains. Sometimes for me it takes a sheer act of will to bless them in their starkness.

They look dead. But of course, in winter the plants are not dead at all, though they may appear so. They are slumbering. They are settling deep inside their brown limbs and resting so that they may burst forth again one day.

There are rhythms to life, just as there are rhythms in nature. I'm a summer girl myself. My soul greens up when surrounded by the burgeoning of life around me. But even I, who dream of eternal summer, know that my enjoyment of it is both heightened by and dependent upon its chillier cousins.

Nature teaches us so many things, and its seasonal lessons should not be ignored. The slumber of winter. The promise of spring. The glory of summer. The bounty of autumn. The rhythms of repose and exultation, starkness and abundance, death and life—it all surrounds us for the ongoing purpose of reminding us the truth about the nature and needs of life.

—*Defiant Joy*, pages 146–148

The signs around us help us to remember that God is present. He is Immanuel, God with us, every season and every moment of our lives. Knowing that our God, who is pure love and the source of our life, is with us can help us to choose love and to choose life even when our circumstances are painfully hard. Choosing to believe can feel hard, but God promises that He is our strength. We too can pray as the man in Mark 9, "I do believe; help me overcome my unbelief!"

1. What promises surround you these days?

    Despite Corona, we still have promises

2. What hard are you facing right now in the midst of the signs?

3. Is there a different hard that you can choose?

    Attitude could be bad
    Choose to have joy
    or be down in
    the dumps.

4. Look up John 10:10. Write it here.

    The thief cometh not to rome
    but to kill, steal, + destroy
    But I have come that ye might
    have life + life more abundantly.

We live in a fallen world with an enemy that would like to destroy us. And we live in a world where Jesus has come to rescue us and bring us life. The abundant life that Jesus promised is available to us right in the middle of what may feel like a frozen landscape.

Because of Jesus, we can dare to risk to hope.

5. To dare to risk hope, we have to look at the track record of our Father. What has He done? *Everything* —

6. Read the following Scriptures and write a word that describes what God has done for you.

Colossians 1:13 —

John 3:16 *For God so loved the world that He gave His only begotten Son that whosoever believeth in Him should have not known but eternal life*

2 Timothy 1:9 —

Ephesians 1:3 —

7. What has He personally done for you? Where have you experienced His faithfulness? *Saved me. Always with me. even when going through tough times Over + over*

Read aloud John 14:1–3:

"Do not let your hearts be troubled. You believe in God; believe also in me. My Father's house has many rooms; if that were not so, would I have told you that I am going there to prepare a place for you? And if I go and prepare a place for you, I will come back and take you to be with me that you also may be where I am."

Our Jesus has suffered in every way that we suffer. He is acquainted with grief. And there is not a moment of your life—not even in the moment of your passing on to heaven—that you are alone. You have a faithful companion who goes before you, behind you, and within you, who promises to never leave you or forsake you. Who has promised that He has suffered in ways you never will so that you will have eternal life—the life that you have always wanted and were born to. Where your every longing will be fulfilled and your every dream will come true.

—*Defiant Joy*, pages 149–150

Your future rests securely in the heart of God. He is your future. You get HIM. Increasingly. More and more, day in and day out. He will not be held back. The Creator of creation refuses to allow the suffering of these days to prevent Him from being known by you in such a way that your heart is held steady, assured, comforted, and filled with hope. Though the seasons of our lives shift and give way to new ones that we welcome or question, our faithful God never shifts. He never changes. Our eyes can look to Him and in doing so, we can rest.

8. Look up 1 Peter 1:13 and write it here.

Gird your mind . . .

9. Where is your hope to be placed? With your hope fully placed there, how would it affect your life when storms come your way?

In J. Christ

Heaven: It's REAL!

> We received Christ by faith, and we are meant to enjoy Him utterly. We are meant to know and experience joy and live with the vibrant hope of the glory that is going to be revealed when Jesus returns. Dear ones, He is returning. Say it out loud. Remind yourself.
>
> We can live with a defiant joy because our happily ever after is on its way. In Jesus our life is unending and, at the renewal of all things, the life we long for is coming.
>
> —*Defiant Joy*, page 158

10. What are the first three things you'd like to do when you get to heaven? Let your imagination run wild!

- *Be embraced by the Lord*
- *See my parents + grandparents*
- *Be healed completely. See Ike completely healed.*

I wrote in *Defiant Joy* that I had woken up one morning weighed down by worries and things that were going wrong. It is too often the case. That particular morning,

I made a list in my mind to justify my anxious heart. Jesus invited me to make another list. A list of the things I am grateful for. So I did. It was a long list.

> We are called to be thankful in everything. Not *for* everything, but *in* everything. And we must be if we are to experience the deep joy that is meant to dwell in the very center of our being. Thankfulness is the key that opens the door to the joy we are meant to walk in.
>
> A grateful heart is a heart that is free. An ungrateful heart is a heart that is bound. . . .
>
> Gratitude is the key, friends. Gratitude unlocks joy. And to be grateful, we need to remember the reason for our gratitude—we are grateful because we have been rescued.
>
> —*Defiant Joy*, pages 164–165

we are joyful because we know we will spend eternity w/ God

11. To cultivate gratitude, we need to remember and ponder the reasons that we have to be thankful. Because the very best way to cultivate joy is to cultivate a thankful heart. So today, regardless of what is swirling around you or what you may be suffering, write a prayer thanking God for at least three things you are grateful for right now.

12. List the three things you mentioned in your prayer. (Feel free to make your list much longer!)

-
-
-

13. Where has God come through for you? When? How?

14. Look up Nehemiah 8:10 and write it here.

15. What stories could you tell others about the goodness of God?

16. Is there a time or a place that you remember where you encountered God's love in a profound way (perhaps on a certain beach or at a retreat)? Though perhaps not physical, what is the stone of remembrance in your life?

17. What did you come to know more deeply in that experience? (Ex.: His kindness, His provision, His always being there for you)

18. Right here and now, write a Prayer of Gratitude to your faithful King.

Cultivating Joy

It is a great good to discover that we can actively participate with God in increasing the joy we possess in our lives. A fabulous way is to share it with others whether we are feeling it or not. Let me suggest some ways to do that.

- Every day for a week, intentionally smile at a stranger.
- At least once, let someone go in front of you at the grocery store.
- When in a hurry or running late to an appointment, make the conscious choice to breathe, invite God into your moment, and slow down. Literally. If you are driving, slow down.
- Sing. In the car. In the shower. Someplace alone. Let your voice rise.
- When you wake, before you begin your day, tell God what you are thankful for.

WORSHIP SONG

Pick any one of them—or all of them! Put it (them) on repeat! Find a time to listen when you are not distracted by many other things. Bless you.

- "Build My Life" – Housefires
- "So Will I" – 100 Billion X
- "You Are Mine" – Mosaic

CONTEMPLATIVE PRAYER

Set apart five minutes or more. Bring your journal with you. Quiet yourself. Ask the Holy Spirit to help you focus on Him. Take a few deep breaths to help center yourself.

Holy Spirit, I center myself in You. I pray that You would fill and guide this time. Help me to remember. I give You my thoughts. I give You my imagination. I give You my memory.

Read this Scripture:

"And Joshua set up at Gilgal the twelve stones they had taken out of the Jordan. He said to the Israelites, 'In the future when your descendants ask their parents, "What do these stones mean?" tell them, "Israel crossed the Jordan on dry ground." For the LORD your God dried up the Jordan before you until you had crossed over. The LORD your God did to the Jordan what he had done to the Red Sea when he dried it up before us until we had crossed over. He did this so that all the peoples of the earth might know that the hand of the LORD is powerful and so that you might always fear the LORD your God.'" (Joshua 4:20-24)

Now, remember a time and a place that you experienced God's love for you. Picture yourself there.
What did God do?

How did you feel?

It is a holy place in your memory and in your heart. Imagine putting a marker there. A stone of remembrance. What will it be? A literal stone? A cross? A bouquet of flowers? It can be anything you desire.

Thank God for His divine love and intervention in Your life.

Thank You, God, for Your love for me. I adore You. You have been nothing but kind and good to me in every season of my life. You have chosen me, and once again, right now, I choose You. I love You.

The Ultimate Victory

INTRODUCTION

Group leader reads aloud these opening words from Stasi:

The sun is setting over the horizon and the world is ensconced in a rosy glow. The ending of this day is a lovely one. The last rays of light caress the landscape like a kiss. I am not grieved at this ending. The sun rises and the sun falls. This sunset does not speak of finality but merely of a passing. This ending signals the beginning of twilight. The night will come. The stars will emerge. And after many hours, the sun will rise again. It speaks of a truth written deeply into the universe.

We are but flowers that fade too soon. Our partings come to one another unwanted and unbidden. Endings can be so very painful. Good-byes can be excruciating. But they are temporary.

In Christ—and this is our deepest hope, so let me say it again—in Christ, we do not die. We live. We will live again. The sun will rise and so will we. A grand and endless hello is coming.

WATCH VIDEO SESSION 6

Video Notes

Use this space to make note of anything that stands out to you in the teaching.

"Where, O death, is your victory? Where, O death, is your sting?"
(1 Corinthians 15:55)

GROUP DISCUSSION: "LOVING AND LOVED"

Gather into small groups if part of a larger group. Spend time together reacting to what Stasi said in the video through these prompts and questions.

Gathering Together

Read aloud as a group the following Scripture:

"As a prisoner for the Lord, then, I urge you to live a life worthy of the calling you have received. Be completely humble and gentle; be patient, bearing with one another in love." (Ephesians 4:1–2)

Briefly share something you learned from your personal study time.

What jumped out at you or surprised you or struck you most in the video?

1. To grow in love is to grow in JOY. Describe a time in your life when you experienced growth in love that resulted in JOY.

2. Stasi said, "The deepest truth in the universe is that you are LOVED." Say that again to yourself. Take turns in your group, look to the person to your right, and speak this truth over her with honesty and conviction. Then, share what it feels like to have this statement proclaimed over you, to hear the words, "You are LOVED."

3. Where and when has loving others felt risky to you?

4. What has loving others cost you?

5. Have you had to say good-bye to someone in your life? How has that experience left you feeling? Do you consider saying good-bye hopeful? Why or why not?

6. Stasi talked about the phrase *a hui hou*, which means, "I'll see you later." Does that help your heart in any way with the partings you have had to face or know you will be facing in the future? Why or why not?

7. What is your greatest hope?

Group leader reads aloud these words from Stasi:

Our view of the-life-to-come is one of the most important views we hold. We cannot hope for what we have no concept of. Jesus says that when He returns, He will make *all things new* (Revelation 21:5). He doesn't say He will make *all new things*. When the heavenly Jerusalem comes down from heaven, it comes to earth (Revelation 21:2). God does not destroy the earth. The Hebrew word that John uses is *palengenesia*, meaning "Genesis again." The earth will be cleansed, restored, and made new. The Scriptures say that all creation is groaning for the sons and daughters of God "to be revealed" (Romans 8:19).

You will be revealed as the one God had in mind before He created the world. Everything you have struggled with will be utterly gone. Everything your loved ones have struggled with will no longer exist. You will have all God's creation as your playground and workshop. No shame, no sin, no death, and no devil will exist any longer to torment you (Revelation 20:14). You will see Jesus face to face and worship Him with a joy that is inconceivable.

8. So now, what are you truly looking forward to?

9. Take five minutes to sit quietly before our God and thank Him in prayer. Let down your guard and all that keeps you from hoping for the future and the life you have yet to live. Listen. Listen to God. Listen for a word of hope and truth. At the end of the five minutes, share with one another a word or a feeling that came over you as you prayed.

Scripture Response

Ask for volunteers to read each of the following verses/passages aloud to the group. Go around the room and have each woman share one word or phrase that comes to mind after hearing these Scriptures:

> "'Though the mountains be shaken
> and the hills be removed,
> yet my unfailing love for you will not be shaken
> nor my covenant of peace be removed,'
> says the LORD, who has compassion on you." (Isaiah 54:10)

"The Lord himself goes before you and will be with you; he will never leave you nor forsake you. Do not be afraid; do not be discouraged." (Deuteronomy 31:8)

"And hope does not put us to shame, because God's love has been poured out into our hearts through the Holy Spirit, who has been given to us." (Romans 5:5)

CLOSING PRAYER

Leader or volunteer, close your group time in prayer:

Dearest Father,

I know that You who did not spare Your own Son promise will spare no good thing from me. The largest good that I can conceive is the Life that is to come. Father, I pray to dream of it and set my hope there. I give You access to my imagination that I may hope in what is coming more keenly. This world is not my home. You are my Home and when the King of Kings, Jesus, returns in His glory, He will make all things new—including me. You will wipe every tear from my eye. There will be no more sorrow or suffering and no more painful good-byes. O Abba, I truly long for that day. Come back, Jesus! Come back soon.

While I wait and long for Your return, I give You permission to change me into a person who truly loves. I want to be conformed into Your image that I might lay my life down for others. I pray to choose joy as a way to love and to be unwavering in my joy because of all You have won for me and all You have promised me.

You are faithful! You are beautiful! You are magnificent! Your glory is beyond my limited comprehension, and I love You! I adore You, God. I worship You. You alone are worthy of all the love I possess. I pray to love You with my whole heart. I pray to love You with an unwavering joy.

In Jesus' powerful Name I pray,

Amen

Session 6

Personal Study

Read chapters 11–12 in Defiant Joy. *Then, reread the excerpts included here and answer the questions that follow.*

Before we begin this final personal study, I'd like you to go back and briefly review Session 1: A Reason to Celebrate. Where do you need to proclaim and enforce the kingdom of God?

When Adam Lanza opened fire at Sandy Hook Elementary School that fateful day, two of the teachers, Victoria Leigh Soto and Anne Marie Murphy, used their bodies as human shields to protect the children in their care. The *New York Post* reported that the principal of the school, Dawn Hochsprung, "reacted like a lioness protecting her cubs. She ran out of the office and lunged at Lanza—and died when he trained his gun on her and opened fire" (NYPost.com/2012-12-16 heroic-teachers-made-the-ultimate-sacrife-for-kids/).

I am awed and so deeply grateful for valiant hearts like these.

Sacrifice my life? Lay down my desires? I can barely let someone else choose the movie we are going to watch. Sacrifice does not come naturally. Nor does laying down our right to take offense—becoming critical or even miserable—not even when it diminishes another person's opportunity for joy.

Yet Christ calls us to lay our lives down for the benefit of others. We are instructed to die to the self-life—a call so contrary to the times we are living in, it sounds laughable. This is the age of the Offended Self. My way or the highway. Entitlement reigns. Agree with me or bear the consequences of my wrath. People shred one another on social media for the slightest offense. Opinions are spouted as if every opinion matters as much as the next. We judge, and we think it's our right to do so.

God says it isn't. Matthew 7:1 says, "Do not judge, or you too will be judged."

God commands us to love one another, to bear one another's burdens—not add to them. He tells us to put the needs of other people above our own and to, in humility, care for the well-being of the other.

What does that have to do with joy?

Everything.

—*Defiant Joy*, pages 171–172

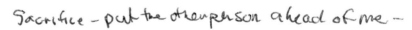

Sacrifice – put the other person ahead of me –

1. Does sacrificing for others come very easily for you?

2. Where do you find it difficult?

3. Where might Jesus be calling you to lay your life down on behalf of others?

> *Our choices to love will either increase or erode the joy of those around us. Much to our surprise, our choices to die to the self-life increase our own joy as well. Dramatically.*

4. Where would you like most to make the choice to love?

5. Look up Matthew 22:39 and write it here.

   " Love your neighbor as yourself."

We know we are commanded to love. What I'd like to point out is that one of the most marvelous ways we love is by choosing to live with joy. Because our choices to love will either increase or erode the joy of those around us. Our choices to pursue a joy-filled life have a snowball effect on those who inhabit our daily world. There are so many reasons for this. For one, it makes us a delight to be around. For another, living with joy is the most enticing way we allure others to God. I'd like to suggest that being a joyful person is one of the key ways you can honor God, love Him, and lay down your life for the benefit of others.

—*Defiant Joy*, page 173

*   *   *

And I know it costs to love. To love another person is to risk being hurt by them. It is THE RISK we are called to make and, really, the one we want to make. We are all made to live in love—to be loved and to love others. That only happens in community.

—Stasi

6. How has loving another person cost you?

7. The first and greatest commandment is to love God with all your heart, mind, soul, and strength (Deuteronomy 6:5; Luke 10:27). Note that the heart comes first. Look up the following verses:

Isaiah 29:13 (What is it that God does not like?)

Forasmuch as this people draw near me w/ their mouth, + w/ their lips do honour me, but have removed their heart far from me

Proverbs 3:5 (How are we to trust God?)

Trust in the Lord + lean not unto thine own understanding

Proverbs 23:26 (What does God want you to give Him?)

My son, give me thine heart

Loving God expresses itself in how we love others. We honor Him by serving others, yes. But clearly, serving God, even obeying His commands from a heart that is far from Him, brings Him no pleasure. His first priority is your heart. He wants your love.

innermost being   *mind, will & emotions*

8. Take a moment and express your love to Jesus. Simply tell Him how much you love Him and a couple of the reasons why. How has He been faithful? Where have you known His goodness? How has He shown His love *to you?*

We give Him our
everything —
like we are
married to them
Guard your mind, etc.

We need to get
in the bottle —
spend time w/ them
pray.
In our mind constantly
It's like He is in you
all the
time.

Our hearts stretch to the bursting point in profound loss, don't they? They expand almost beyond bearing.

It is a sorrow that our Father knows well. *It is a suffering that our Jesus would not spare us from.* It is a pain that is born from loving.

—*Defiant Joy*, page 197

*   *   *

There is a risk to love people. Essentially, it is the risk of losing them. And in this world, we will lose them, either by death or a shift in the relationship. Good-byes are the most painful thing I know. Our hope lies in the fact that our good-byes are temporary.

—Stasi

9. Look up Psalm 56:8. Write it down here.

> *put thou my tears in thy bottle,*
> *are they not in your book*

10. What does this tell you about how God feels about what you endure?

> *He cares*

11. Look up 1 Corinthians 15:55 and read it aloud. Where have you known the sting of death? Right in this place, invite Jesus to come and more fully heal your tender heart.

> *O death, where is thy sting?*
> *O grave, where is thy victory?*

Read 1 Corinthians 15:50–52, 54.

"I declare to you, brothers and sisters, that flesh and blood cannot inherit the kingdom of God, nor does the perishable inherit the imperishable. Listen, I tell you a mystery: We will not all sleep, but we will all be changed—in a flash, in the twinkling of an eye, at the last trumpet. For the trumpet will sound, the dead will be raised imperishable, and we will be changed. . . .

"When the perishable has been clothed with the imperishable, and the mortal with immortality, then the saying that is written will come true: 'Death has been swallowed up in victory.'"

12. Dear one, write it again. What is your ultimate hope?

Go to Heaven

13. The awareness of our heart's longings for life is heightened with every death. Let your heart rise. What are you longing for? Write it down and ask God to come for you in your longings.

14. What gentle invitations are surrounding you these days to help you see that the greatest good, the resurrection, is coming to you?

> Sometimes I have wondered, *How can God be such a joyful person in the face of all the heartbreak in the world?* The answer is because He sees the great restoration as if it were already here.
>
> All around us, gentle invitations of truth and grace call to us, if we will have the ears to hear. Today I do hear, and I am reminded of the promise of the restoration of all things. Death *has* lost its sting. The grave holds *no* victory. My visible world may scream loss, but the victory cannot and will not be held back. And because of that, because life wins and has won already, because of all Jesus has won for us, I—like you—can be defiantly joyful. I will choose it. Join me.
>
> —*Defiant Joy*, page 197

15. In the face of the ultimate reality that Jesus has conquered death forever, do you want to be a woman of unwavering joy? How will you choose it?

Prayer

Dearest God,

Thank You that, though partings are excruciating, in You they are temporary. I need Your help to remember Your goodness in the midst of them. I need to hold on to Your faithfulness and to the ultimate victory that Jesus has won for us. Would You help me to remember? Help me to see Your faithfulness in every moment of my life. O God, deepen the anchor of my soul's hope in the grace that is to be revealed when You return in glory. I long for that day. I pray You make what is coming even more real to me. I need You. I love You. You are my joy.

In Your Name, Jesus, the Name above all names, I pray,
Amen

WORSHIP SONG

Pick any one of them—or all of them! Put it (them) on repeat! Find a time to listen when you are not distracted by many other things. Bless you.

- "You Are Mine" – Mosaic
- "Resurrecting" – Elevation Worship
- "What a Beautiful Name" – Hillsong

CONTEMPLATIVE PRAYER

As this is our last opportunity to practice contemplative prayer as a part of this study, make sure to set aside at least ten minutes so you'll be able to receive all that Jesus has for you.

Turn off your phone. Settle in. Get comfortable.

Pray.

Holy Spirit, I consecrate this time to You and to Your purposes. I sanctify my imagination to the kingdom of God. Please come and meet with me, Lord.

As thoughts and distractions come to your mind, just note them. Tell yourself you will come back to them later. Everyone's mind wanders. Just breathe. In fact, take several deep breaths. Breathe in deeply and breathe out slowly three times.

Come, Jesus.

Start by reading John 20:15–16:

"[Jesus] asked her, 'Woman, why are you crying? Who is it you are looking for?'

"Thinking he was the gardener, she said, 'Sir, if you have carried him away, tell me where you have put him, and I will get him.'

"Jesus said to her, 'Mary.'

"She turned toward him and cried out in Aramaic, 'Rabboni!' (which means 'Teacher')."

Imagine yourself in a garden. Look around. Drink in the beauty. Picture it as vividly as you can. It turns out it is not just any garden; it is *the* garden. It is Easter morning, and the sun has just broken over the horizon. You are there with the other women who have come to anoint Jesus' body, but when you arrived, you found the stone had been rolled away.

Where is your Lord? How do you feel?

You see the gardener and you run to him. You ask him, *"Do you know where they have taken my Lord?"*

In response, the "gardener" says your name. He gently, lovingly, with all the kindness of the Godhead, says *your* name. At the sound of your name whispered from His lips, you recognize the Risen King.

And you fall at His feet.

Worship Him.

Tell Him all that is in your heart. All that you are thankful for. All that you are in awe of. All that you are longing for. All the hope that you have and all the hope that you need. Ask Him to come for you in every way that you so need Him to come.

And Amen. Bless you, friend.

"[A]nd those the LORD has rescued will return.
They will enter Zion with singing;
    everlasting joy will crown their heads.
Gladness and joy will overtake them,
    and sorrow and sighing will flee away." (Isaiah 35:10)

Leader's Guide

Thank you for your willingness to lead your group through *Unwavering: Living with Defiant Joy*. The rewards of leading are different from the rewards of participating, and we hope you find your own walk with Jesus deepened by this experience. This leader's guide will give you some tips on how to prepare for your time together and facilitate a meaningful experience for your group members.

WHAT DOES IT TAKE TO LEAD THIS STUDY?

Get together and watch God show up. Seriously, that's the basics of how a small group works. Gather several people together who have a hunger for God, want to learn more about what is available for them in the here and now, and are willing to be open and honest with God and themselves. The Lord will honor this every time and show up in the group. You don't have to be a pastor, priest, theologian, or counselor to lead a group through this study. Just invite people over, watch the video, and talk about it. All you need is a willing heart, a little courage, and God will do the rest. Really.

HOW THIS STUDY WORKS

There are three important pieces to the *Unwavering* small-group study: (1) the book *Defiant Joy: Taking Hold of Hope, Beauty, and Life in a Hurting World*, (2) the six-session video study, and (3) this study guide. Make sure everyone in your group has a copy of the book and a study guide. It works best if you can get books and guides to your group *before* the first meeting. That way, everyone can read the first two chapters ahead of time and be prepared to watch the first video session together. The study guide is written in such a way that participants do not have to read the book to participate; however, their experience will be much richer if they do. There is a section for the group to do together and there is a section to help participants go deeper into the material on their own during the following week. To do that, they will need to read the book.

This series is presented in six video sessions, with each session approximately twenty minutes in length. Each week, you'll meet together to watch the video and discuss the session. This series can also be used in classroom settings, such as Sunday school classes, though you may need to modify the discussion time depending on the size of the class. You could even use the video as sessions for a special retreat.

Basically, each week you and your group will:

1. Watch the video session together.
2. Talk about it.
3. Answer the questions found in this guide about the video.
4. Those who are going deeper will then read the corresponding chapters in *Defiant Joy* and work through the personal study.
5. Depending on your group, you may want to talk about what struck them in the chapters as well.

That's it!

A FEW TIPS FOR LEADING A GROUP

- *The setting really matters.* If you can choose to meet in a living room over a conference room in a church, do it. Pick an environment that's conducive to people relaxing and getting real. Remember, the enemy likes to distract us when it comes to prayer and seeking God, so do what you can to remove these obstacles from your group (silence cell phones, limit background noise, no texting). Set the chairs or couches in a circle to prevent having a "classroom" feel.

- *Have some refreshments!* Coffee and water will do; cookies and snacks are even better. People tend to be nervous when they join a new group, so if you can give them something to hold onto (like a warm mug of coffee), they will relax a lot more. It's human nature.

- *Good equipment is important.* Meet where you can watch the video sessions on a screen big enough for everyone to see and enjoy. Get or borrow the best gear you can. Also, be sure to test your media equipment ahead of time to make sure everything is in working condition. This way, if something isn't working, you can fix it or make other arrangements before the meeting begins. (You'll be amazed at how the enemy will try to mess things up for you!)

- *Be honest.* Remember that your honesty will set the tone for your time together. Be willing to answer questions personally, as this will set the pace for the length of your group members' responses and will make others more comfortable in sharing.

- *Stick to the schedule.* Strive to begin and end at the same time each week. The people in your group are busy, and if they can trust you to be a good steward of their time, they will be more willing to come back each week. Of course, you want to be open to the work God is doing in the group members as they are challenged to reconsider some of their preconceived ideas about the availability of the kingdom of God to bring them joy in their everyday lives, and at times you may want to *linger* in prayer or discussion. Remember the clock serves *you*; your group doesn't serve the clock. But work to respect the group's time, especially when it comes to limiting the discussion times.

- *Don't be afraid of silence or emotion.* Welcome awkward moments. The material presented during this study will likely bring to the surface areas of pain and suffering. Don't be afraid to ease into the material with the group to allow space for honoring one another's stories and personal questions.

- *Don't dominate the conversation.* Even though you are the leader, you are also a member of this small group. So don't steamroll over others in an attempt to lead—and don't let anyone else in the group do so either.

- *Prepare for your meeting.* Watch the video for the meeting ahead of time. Though it may feel a bit like cheating because you'll know what's coming, you'll be better prepared for what the session might stir in the hearts of your group members. Also review the material in this guide and be sure to spend time in prayer. In fact, the *most important* thing you can do is simply pray ahead of time each week:

> *Lord Jesus, come and rule this time. Let Your Spirit fill this place. Bring Your kingdom here. Take us right to the things we really need to talk about and rescue us from every distraction. Show us the heart of the Father. Meet each person here. Give us Your grace and love for one another. In Your Name I pray.*

- *Make sure your group members are prepared.* Before the first meeting, secure enough copies of the study guide and the *Defiant Joy* book for each member. Have these ready and on hand for the first meeting, or make sure the participants have purchased these resources for themselves. Send out a reminder email or a text a couple of days before the meeting to make sure folks don't forget about it.

AS YOU GATHER

You will find the following counsel to be especially helpful when you meet for the first time as a group. I offer these comments in the spirit of "here is what I would do if I were leading a group through this study."

First, as the group gathers, start your time with introductions if people don't know each other. Begin with yourself and share your name, how long you've been a follower of Christ, if you have a spouse and/or children, and what you want to learn most about the stance of defiant joy. Going first will put the group more at ease.

After each person has introduced herself, share—in no more than five minutes—what your hopes are for the group. Then jump right into watching the video session, as this will help get things started on a strong note. In the following weeks you will then want to start by allowing folks to catch up a little—say, fifteen minutes or so—with some "hey, so how are you?" kind of banter. Too much of this burns up your meeting time, but you have to allow some room for it because it helps build relationships among the group members.

Note that each group will have its own personality and dynamics. Typically, people will hold back the first week or two until they feel the group is "safe." Then they will begin to share. Again, don't let it throw you if your group seems a bit awkward at first. Of course, some people *never* want to talk, so you'll need to coax them out as time goes on. But let it go the first week.

INSIGHT FOR DISCUSSION

If the group members are in any way open to talking about their lives as it relates to this material, you will *not* have enough time for every question suggested in this study guide. That's okay! Pick the questions ahead of time that you know you want to cover, just in case you end up only having time to discuss a few of them.

You set the tone for the group. Your honesty and vulnerability during discussion times will tell them what they can share. How *long* you talk will give them an example of how long they should. So give some thought to what stories or insights from your own work in the study guide you want to highlight.

WARNING: The greatest temptation for most small group leaders is to add to the video teaching with a little "teaching session" of their own. This is unhelpful for three reasons:

1. The discussion time will be the richest time during your meeting. The video sessions have been intentionally kept short so you can have plenty of time for discussion. If you add to the teaching, you sacrifice this precious time.
2. You don't want your group members *teaching*, *lecturing*, or *correcting* one another. Every person is at a different place in her spiritual journey—and

that's good. But if you set a tone by teaching, the group will feel like they have the freedom to teach one another. That can be disastrous for group dynamics.

3. The participants will have watched the video teaching and possibly read the corresponding chapters in *Defiant Joy*. They don't need more content! They want a chance to talk and process their own lives in light of all they have taken in.

A STRONG CLOSE

Some of the best learning times will take place after the group time as God brings new insights to the participants during the week. Encourage group members to write down any questions they have as they read through *Defiant Joy* and do the preparation work. Make sure they know you are available for them as they explore what God has to say about any of the concepts that might be new or challenging to them. Finally, make sure you close your time by praying together. Perhaps ask two or three people to pray, inviting God to fill your group and lead each person during this study. (A closing prayer is included in the guide, should you want to use it instead of or in addition to extemporaneous prayer.)

Thank you again for taking the time to lead your group. May God reward your efforts and dedication and make your time together in *Unwavering: Living with Defiant Joy* fruitful for His kingdom.